Heaven
on
Earth

CHIARA LUBICH

Heaven On Earth

Meditations and Reflections

New City Press

Published in the United States by New City Press
202 Cardinal Rd., Hyde Park, NY 12538
www.newcitypress.com
©2000 New City Press

Translated from Italian by Jerry Hearne
© Città Nuova, Rome, Italy

Cover design by Nick Cianfarani

Library of Congress Cataloging-in-Publication Data:
Lubich, Chiara, 1920-
Heaven on earth : meditations and reflections / Chiara Lubich.
    p. cm.
Translated from Italian.
ISBN 1-56548-144-5
1. Meditations. 2. Christian life--Catholic authors. I. Title.

BX2182.2 .L8118 2000
242--dc21   00-041818

Printed in Canada

Contents

Introduction

Focolare. An unfamiliar word to many in the English-speaking world. In Italian it means "hearth" or "fireplace." Like the French term *foyer*, which also refers to a hearth, *focolare* conveys a sense of gathering, bonding, the warmth of close relationship often evoked by the fireplace.

The term "Focolare" is also the name of a religious movement within the Roman Catholic Church, a spiritual family whose vitality and influence extend well beyond the Church. This movement with its distinctive spirituality has its roots in the life of Chiara Lubich who, in her early twenties, had embarked on a teaching career. Amidst the destruction and horror of World War II Italy, she was seized and saturated by the gift of God's love. In response to that gift she gave her life completely and without reserve to the God whose name above all names is Love (1 Jn 4:8).

Her singular commitment, at first without religious vows or support of a community, altered the course of Chiara's life, and it has changed the lives of countless others. Chiara encouraged others to recognize the magnitude of God's love even and especially in the midst of violence and division. Drawn by her words and to her way of life, the first few made a commitment similar to hers. Those who joined her set out to putting into practice the words of the gospel, sharing their efforts and new understanding as they were nourished and sustained in the bonds of the One Love. Thus were the seeds of the Focolare Movement sown in the soil of the war-torn Italian city of Trent.

As with other founders and foundresses of religious movements in the Church, Chiara Lubich had no idea of how far-reaching would be the fruits of her yes to Love's Word. She simply put her life in the hands of God and followed in faith, by hope, through love.

From its origins in a simple yet total response to Love, the Focolare Movement has spread to 182 countries. Those with a formal commitment to the mission and spirituality of the Movement number 140,000. Over 2 million people are part of the larger family of Focolare, drawing strength from the springs of its spirituality. Thus, "Focolare" is a name that describes men and women, single and married, lay, vowed religious, clergy, Catholic and non-Catholic, from different races, lands, languages, and economic backgrounds, all of whom seek to live by Love and for Love so that all may be brought into a communion in the One Love. Their life is in service of unity between and among nations, races, classes, and creeds — working little by little for the transformation of the world by none other than Love itself.

Three features of the Focolare Movement make it a particularly fitting expression of gospel living in today's Church and in the wider world. These may also help to explain the Movement's appeal to so many people. First, Focolare is a *lay* movement. Even prior to the Second Vatican Council's affirmation of the universal call to holiness (cf. *Lumen gentium*, chapter 5), Chiara Lubich saw clearly that each and every one baptized into the Body of Christ is called to the fullness of holiness. No doubt discerning a crucially important prompting of the Spirit of God at work in the Church and world prior to the Second Vatican Council, she recognized that whatever one's state in life — be one a vowed religious, member of the clergy, or lay person, married or single — one and all are called to the same holiness. And this holiness lies in the perfection of charity. So even while clergy and religious are part of the Movement, it is lay in orientation and spirit. Those who are committed to the Focolare and are active in its work understand themselves first and foremost to be members of the People of God, called to be and become a sign of reconciliation and unity amidst an increasingly divided Church and a broken and wounded world.

Secondly, as expressed in its very name, the Focolare Movement has a strong sense of *community*. Theirs is a profoundly communal spirit of equality, reciprocity and interdependence. The members of Focolare are joined together by a shared vision, a commonly-held sense of meaning, purpose and values. They share in life's joys and sorrows in a spirit of mutual support and service, bonded and bonding together in the One Love.

One of the great riches of the Focolare is its ability

11

to allow a strong communal sensibility to be expressed in a wide range of life forms. Some have formal commitments within the Movement and live an explicit and intentional communal life. Others live their commitment within the context of the basic community of marriage and family. Still others are engaged in a variety of works which, to a greater or lesser degree, further the mission of the Movement. Religious Sisters, Brothers, and priests are enriched by the spirit of community at the heart of the Movement, and are thereby better able to build stronger bonds of community within their own religious institutes and parishes. Yet others have no formal ties to the Movement but share in its spirit and understand themselves to be part of the community in a much wider sense. This rich diversity of configurations of the communal spirit of the Focolare is itself a testament to the magnitude of God's love.

Thirdly, the Focolare Movement is shaped by an ecumenical and interreligious spirit. With roots long, deep, and strong in the Roman Catholic Church, Chiara Lubich quickly recognized that the call of the Focolare Movement is to cultivate, nurture, and sustain the desire for unity in the One Love, wherever it might be found. Thus, not only does the Movement welcome those of other Christian traditions, but those of other faiths as well. Further, included in those who are counted as part of the larger Focolare community are those who profess no creed at all, but who recognize the gift and the task of building a world united in the One Love. At the heart of the Focolare Movement, then, there is a deep spirit of respect for the other, indeed reverence for otherness and difference, in furthering the mission of Christ and the Spirit: "That they may all be one" (John 17:21).

The distinctive spirituality of the Focolare is expressed in the many works of the Movement. Notable among these are the Movement's various publishing enterprises. In the United States, New City Press renders an extraordinary service by making available first-rate theological studies, books with an ecumenical focus, and a rich range of materials aimed at furthering the dialogue between and among people of different faiths. It is a cause for great delight that New City Press is now publishing these reflections and meditations in fresh translation. They will serve as a worthy companion to Chiara Lubich's *Christian Living Today*, or they may stand on their own either as an introduction or a source for deepening the spirituality of the Focolare.

It is a singular pleasure for me to introduce these writings to those in the English-speaking world who may not be familiar with this exceptional woman and her work. Chiara Lubich's accolades and awards are beyond counting here. To name just a few: She is the recipient of the Templeton Prize for Religion, the 1996 UNESCO Peace Education Prize, and was named Religious Author of the Year at the 1995 Milan Book Fair. Her *Christian Living Today* has sold over 600,000 copies worldwide. Yet with all this and so much more, like the Focolare Movement which she founded, Chiara Lubich is hardly a household word. Her name is rarely, if ever, on any of the road signs of today's spirituality superhighway. This is because Chiara's spirituality and the spirit of the Focolare Movement is more discrete, simple and, above all, enduring.

In these pages we are invited to drink from the spiritual sources which have nourished her own life and the lives of millions of others. Hers is a spirituality which is catholic through and through, particularly appropriate to lay people in today's Church and world. This spirituality is first and finally a participation in the mission of Christ and the Spirit, a whole way of living by which we are brought through the superabundance of God's love into a communion in the One Love.

Michael Downey
Professor of Systematic Theology and Spirituality
Saint John's Seminary, Camarillo
Author of *Hope Begins Where Hope Begins*

Only One
Great Love

God Is Love

You have been blinded with me by the fiery brilliance of an ideal that exceeds all things and contains all: the infinite love of God. It is he, my God and your God, who has established a bond between us that is stronger than death. . . . It is Love who has called us to love.

It is Love who has spoken in the depths of our hearts and told us, "Look around you. Everything in the world passes away. Every day sees its evening, and how quickly each evening comes. . . . Love what does not die. Love the one who is love."

Love always. All people are created to love.

Yes, there is suffering in this world. But for the one who loves, suffering is nothing; even martyrdom is a song; even the cross is a song. God is love!

The Coming of the Sun

The presence of love in the world
is like the coming of the sun in springtime.
The arid and barren earth
with seemingly nothing to offer,
suddenly turns green and begins to blossom.
The seeds were there all the time,
but the warmth they needed was missing.
Similarly, the world is full of good intentions
    and good will.
But often these don't produce the desired fruits,
because the warmth of love is not there to ripen them.

What Remains

> "Love never fails. There are in the end three things that last: faith, hope, and love, and the greatest of these is love" (1 Cor 13:8.13).

This is the reason we need to be love in a total way, to do everything with love. This will lead us on the path to eternal life. To place ourselves into love is placing ourselves into what remains: God. It is God whom we want to chose moment by moment as the one and all of our lives.

Holy scripture puts it splendidly: "Love the Lord your God with all your heart, with all your soul, with all your strength. The commandments I give you today are to be written on your heart. You shall repeat and speak of them to your children whether at rest in your house or walking abroad, at your lying down or at your rising. Fasten them on your hand as a sign and wear them on the forehead as a phylactery. Write them on the doorposts of your house and on your gates" (Dt 6:5-9).

For Me

Speaking of Jesus, Paul writes, " . . . and he gave his life for me" (Rom 5:8). Each of us can repeat those words of the apostle: *for me*.

My Jesus,
you have died for me,
how can I doubt your mercy?
And if I can believe in that mercy with a faith
that teaches me that God has died for me,
how can I not risk everything to return such love?

For me . . .
Words that wipe away the solitude of the most lonely
and give divine value
to every person despised by the world.
Words that fill every heart and make it overflow
upon those who either do not know
or do not remember the Good News.

For me.
For me, Jesus, all those sufferings?
For me that cry on the cross?

Surely, you will never give up on us.
You will do everything imaginable to save us
if only because we have cost you so much.

You gave me divine life
just as my mother gave me human life.
In every moment
you think of me alone,
as you do of each and every person.
This — more than anything in the world —
gives us the courage to live as Christians.

For me. Yes, for me.

And so, Lord,
for the years that remain,
allow me also to say:
for you.

That Was How I Found You

L ord,
    when they speak of love,
most people perhaps think of something
that is always the same.
Yet, how varied love is!

Lord,
I remember how I met you.
I didn't worry then about how to love you.
Maybe because it was *you* who came to *me*,
and *you* who took care to fill *my* heart.
I remember virtually burning with love for you.
Certainly I felt the dragging burden of my humanity,
but through your grace
I understood already then
a little of who I was and who you were.
I understood that the flame in my heart
was your gift.

Then you showed me a way to find you.
"Under the cross, under every cross,"
you would tell me, "I am there.
Embrace it and you will find me."
You said this to me many times.
While I don't remember your reasoning,

I do know that you convinced me.
As each suffering arrived, I thought of you,
and with my will I said yes.
The cross, however, remained:
an inner darkness, a heartrending pain
— how many crosses in our life!

But later on you taught me
to love you in my brothers and sisters.
From then on, faced with any kind of suffering,
I did not stop but, accepting it,
turned to the person next to me,
without thinking of myself any longer.
And after a while, during a moment of reflection,
I would find that my sorrow had disappeared.
And so it was for years and years:
a continuing exercise in accepting the cross
and the asceticism of love.
Trials came and went.
You know about them.
You who count even the hairs of my head,
certainly have placed those trials in your heart too.
Now love is different;
it is no longer only a result of will-power.

I knew that God is love.
But I did not imagine him quite this way.

Penance, Old and New

Ours are not times known for penance. On the contrary, penance is often viewed as an obscure tradition of a distant past.

Instead, what comes to the forefront in our age is love. And this because God is love.

The starting point of a person's conversion today is often belief in love, which brings a new flow of life. Faith in God's love opens our eyes. We see other people, things, and circumstances as signs of his love, and everything becomes clearer.

Then it becomes easy to respond to all that love asks and desires; it is almost impossible not to. Thus, God's commandments become our means to respond with love to his love.

Moreover, we become aware that suffering is something sacred, which cannot be rejected but needs to be welcomed and even desired. We realize that it is through suffering that God has shown his love to us, and that through suffering and self-denial we can return his love. The need for penance emerges anew, but with a different meaning. . . .

We should certainly be open to change and to healthy renewal, but whichever way we look at it, we should keep in mind that God is love — a love that went as far as being crucified for us.

The One and Only Great Love

Living Christianity authentically consists in loving God with all our strength and, in him, loving all created beings — and these two in the right order.

Sometimes we may get it wrong. Moving to the second point too quickly, we misinterpret it.

What we need to do is to love *God*, giving him our whole being: our time, our work, our love, our intellect. To express this, it is also necessary to turn our attention, care and love to those he has created. But we need to do this only for *him*, in order to continue loving him. We should be perennial contemplatives. Alas, how often we fail!

What freedom we would find, however, in this one and only great love. Just thinking of it makes us feel freed from the countless bonds which social life imposes on us.

The "One Thing Necessary"

The change that the world is unknowingly awaiting from us, the "revolution" that every Christian should carry out, is nothing other than bringing one's life to inner unity.

We might lead a life that is good, yet somehow colorless and dull, lacking in drive. One thing follows the other without much meaning. We go to work, stop for coffee, catch the train, come home to watch TV, sit down to eat, perhaps visit some friends. We won't forget to attend Sunday Mass or even to perform a good deed.

But this kind of Christianity no longer attracts today's men and women, whose interests lie in space flights and science, and whose thoughts accompany their heads of state to summit meetings where the fate of the world and its peoples is decided. Nor does it have much to say to one who lives for daily pleasures or pursues some degree of artistic expression. Nor to workers who fight for great ideals and struggle for social justice.

Many Christians today need to experience a new conversion. We need to root our lives in the only thing that is necessary. Then everything else will fall into place. This "one thing necessary" is the love of God. If we love him wholeheartedly, if we let him take root in our hearts, if everyone will adore him and serve him, then the life of individuals and society will be imbued with his presence. Art and apostolic activity, studies and vacations, family and school, leisure time and illness will all become verses of one song, part of a single, manifold witness we bear to God.

We owe the world only this, and only this should we be concerned with. Then through us God will again be in fashion in this world which, judging from the widespread interest raised by the Second Vatican Council, is not as "worldly" as it may seem.

Give Glory to God

"I glorified you on earth, having accomplished the work which you gave me to do" (Jn 17:4).

This verse shows us how we too can give glory to the Father. To give glory to God is after all our greatest desire. Now we understand: Living for God's glory doesn't consist so much in putting aside our own, cutting back our pride or vainglory, but rather in carrying out the work that God has entrusted to us, until the day he calls us to himself.

God has a plan for each of us; and this plan must be brought to completion.

It Is Love That Counts

Pope Paul VI, in a talk given to the bishops of Oceania, says that love is the core virtue that the world awaits from the Church today. If this is true, and it is true, to respond to the needs of the Church and to the demands of our world we need to be love made concrete.

Love, true love, is our focus in life, knowing well that all things have value if they are inspired and carried out by love, while without love nothing has value, at least not in life's final analysis. If this is our focus, we will be able to say of each of our actions, this will remain. This holds true for our work, as it does for our relaxation, for educating our children, for our conversations with others, our travels, our way of dressing, our manner of eating, and for any other smallest of actions. It holds true for all the unexpected things that each day brings, the surprises God has in store for us. It even holds true — and this is very consoling — if an illness forces us to inactivity and confines us to bed with no apparent end in sight.

It is a truth often mentioned but equally forgotten that what matters is not so much *what* we do or are capable of doing (even in apostolic endeavors) but *how* we do it. Our life should be animated by love. Our actions in themselves are of no importance to God.

What counts is love, the love that keeps the world going. The more our actions are animated by love, the more fruitful they will be.

However, we must remember that all love is not the same. The love distilled from a shred of life that is giving itself like Christ on the cross is surely stronger than the love of one who offers — and certainly everything is to be offered — the joyful and serene things that life holds.

So, if we Christians do not want to be behind the times, we must put love into everything we do. And we need to be especially vigilant that we are not lacking in love when life proves most difficult and painful.

Life That Remains

A sudden misfortune reminds us of the words of scripture, "Everything is vanity of vanities" (Eccl 1:2). Yes, everything passes: people, health, beauty, possessions. God alone remains.

Misfortunes *can* mark the time for us to choose God anew as the one and all of our life, and thus live the way he commands: to love.

When you love, you understand many things, and you will see how the golden thread of your life, at first apparently interrupted, continues to shine as brightly and even more so than before. In our lives we might experience all kinds of disruptions, but the life of God is always alive, and so it is in those who have grafted themselves over and over onto him.

One Logical Choice

"Cursed is the man who trusts in human beings. . . . Blessed is the man who trusts in the Lord" (Jer 17:5.7).

We need more trust in God. This is why we should stop our inner monologues and look for an ever deeper and more intimate dialogue with the Lord. To him we can entrust all that we are and all that we have.

Our trust should become stronger every day. Isn't trusting in God the most sensible thing to do anyway? But our God-given freedom leaves us a choice: to believe or not to believe in love, in God. For someone who has faith, however, such choice seems to be absurd. Because if God exists and if he is love, then there is only one logical choice: to trust in him completely.

United

in

God's Will

Be Vigilant

In order to love God we need to do his will. But his will presents itself one moment at a time. It may be expressed by external circumstances, by our responsibilities, by some advice from more experienced people. . . . Or even by unexpected events, be these sorrowful or delightful, annoying or indifferent.

God's will can be understood only by one who is attentive and vigilant. This is why the gospel speaks so often of vigilance.

The gospel directs us toward the present. It tells us not to worry about the future, to ask the Father only for our daily bread. Jesus invites us to carry today's cross and says that each day has trouble enough of its own. And he warns us that "Once the hand is laid on the plough, no one who looks back is fit for the kingdom of God" (Lk 9:62).

To get used to living the present well, we Christians must know how to forget the past and how not to worry about the future. This is only common sense: After all, the past no longer exists and the future will be when it becomes present. Catherine of Siena said: "The burden of the past we don't have, because time has gone by. The burden of the future we don't have either, because we can't be sure that we will have that time."

Great persons and saints know this principle. They are used to discerning God's voice from among the various inner voices. And with practice it becomes easier, also because God's voice becomes stronger and amplified.

At the start it might be more difficult. First we need to learn how to trust in God, to believe in his love, and to do with determination what we think is his will. We can be confident that he will bring us back on track, should we end up going astray. And even when God's will seems to be clear, calling us for example to do a job that will take hours, there is always a temptation to overcome, a scruple to drive away, some worry to entrust to the heart of God, wandering thoughts to steer away from, desires to say no to.

Living the present is a practice that is extraordinarily rich. It grafts our earthly life already now into eternity.

If We Are United

I f we are united to God in his will, we are also united
among ourselves. It cannot be otherwise. First of
all because unity among us is nothing other than the
result of our personal union with God. Furthermore,
if our unity has become faint, God's will wants us to
rebuild it as soon as possible. We would not even be
Christians if we were to forget this.

The Path to Eternity

God's will is ever new and always creative. It is the eternal path upon which our soul finds peace and balance to continue along its way.

* * *

Who can ever express the infinite beauty, the continuous surprises, the endless horizons contemplated by those who abandon themselves to the divine adventure of God's will!

King of My Heart

Out of habit we often say short prayers like "My God and my all" or "I love you with all my heart." However, as we examine our lives throughout the day to see if we have put God and his will first, we realize that these words do not always correspond to reality.

Oftentimes, we may linger over something we are doing instead of moving on promptly to the next task. Unfortunately, that means that what we are currently doing (reading, meeting someone, watching the news) means more to us than God.

Here we understand where the failures can lie for those who have given themselves to God. Doing his will is the measure. If God's will is first and foremost for me, if it reigns over all else, even over those things I can and should love, then God is truly the king of my heart. If, instead, I thrust aside God's will and allow other things, persons or ideas to reign in its place, then God is like a king dethroned from my heart by my ego.

God's Work Completed

Jesus said that he had completed the work the Father had given him to do (cf. Jn 17:4). He saved us, and he founded his Church that would continue his work. On earth, however, he saw neither the initial expansion of the Church nor its later successes. Yet, he said that he had completed his work.

We often think in human terms about what God might want to achieve through us. We set up goals to reach, not realizing that the history of humanity and of each individual are in *his* hands.

Therefore, we should joyfully "resign" ourselves to fulfilling his plan. Nothing is more beautiful than what God has planned for us. In case we had hoped to accomplish more, let us be in solidarity with those who will continue after us and develop what we were only able to begin. There are "those who sow and others who reap" (Jn 4:37), but both share in the joy.

Our Neighbor:
A Way to God

The Pearl

Today, many people thirst for God. They are seeking a way to transcend their human condition and oftentimes search outside of Christianity.

In the gospel, however, we can find a pearl, suggested by the Holy Spirit for our times. A way to reach God, to find union with him.

We know that throughout the centuries, many exceptional people, saints, have arisen in the Church, and they are considered saints precisely because they succeeded in attaining union with God. But in which way and at what price? To facilitate their relationship with the Lord present in their hearts, they would often withdraw from the world and isolate themselves in the desert or retreat to convents protected by walls, far from the temptations of the world.

But our times require other forms, and the Holy Spirit adapts to these changes. Today, as Igino Giordani once said, sanctity must extend beyond the convent walls and be present in homes, schools, town squares, offices, and in the political arena, because the lay faithful too are called to sanctity.

So being, how can someone who does not live in solitude, is not protected by walls, and does not dispose of the means once required by spiritual life, find union with God? Not only are lay people unprotected, but they are always surrounded by others, while in the past solitude was preferred.

This is where the "pearl" comes into the picture. The Holy Spirit helped us to understand that our neighbor — our brothers and sisters, considered as obstacles in the past — can become our very way to God, a door, a passageway, an opening that leads to union with him.

On one condition, of course: that it not be them to exert a sometimes negative influence on us, but that it be us to influence them with our behavior. How can this be done? We know the answer: By loving them, loving them one by one during the day, the whole day long. By loving them with that "art of loving" which is divine, because it is possible only through the love poured into our hearts by the Holy Spirit.

It is an art we learn from the Gospel. It demands that we love everyone, making no distinction between the pleasant and the unpleasant, the attractive and the unattractive, the fellow countryman and the stranger, the white, the black, the yellow, the European and the American, the African and the Asian. Love knows no discrimination. Christians, furthermore, love everyone, because it is Christ who is loved in each person. He himself said, "You did it to me" (Mt 25:40).

The art of loving requires that one take the initiative without waiting to be loved, that one love the other as oneself. Gandhi used to say, "You and I are but one thing. I cannot harm the other without hurting myself." The art of loving also demands that we learn how to "make ourselves one" with others, that is, that we make their burdens, their concerns, their sufferings, their joys, our own.

What is going to happen if we do this? When we pray in the evening or find a moment for recollection alone with God during the day, we will become aware of his presence. He comes to us because we reached out to him in our brothers and sisters. Thus we experience a union hard to define, perhaps because it is something new, a union perceived by the senses of the soul, and which fills our hearts with love. In his presence, we can work everything out with him.

Moreover, since this union is the consequence of having loved our brothers and sisters, they appear to be not only our beneficiaries, but our benefactors too: They have made our greatest hopes come true. Therefore, we should approach them with gratitude, and this will keep us humble, a virtue very important in loving. . . .

With this special union with God, we will be charged with divine energy and able to keep on reaching out to other neighbors with a love that is always more sensitive, more focused, and more sublime. We will speed toward the goal we have set for ourselves: union with God and union with our brothers and sisters, until all will be one (cf. Jn 17:21).

But it requires giving value to and treasuring the pearl God has given us, the specific way to reach him: our brothers and sisters.

This is a new way, a way for our times.

Our Way to God

"He who does not love his brother whom he
has seen cannot love God whom he has never
seen" (1 Jn 4:20).

O ur pathway to God is our brothers and sisters.
Especially in our times, we should be aware of
this.

Oftentimes we do not pay enough attention to our
neighbors' needs. We let ourselves be trapped by our
materialistic environment with its enticements, by
gossip and idle talk, by our constant need to know, to
be informed, to read everything. . . . Instead, what
really matters is something quite different: "Before
all else have mutual and continual love" (1 Pt 4:8),
and scripture says further, "We have passed out of
death and *into life*. . . because we love our brothers" (1
Jn 3:14).

God calls us to life, and life is what we need to
share with others. To love one's neighbor demands
continual effort. But it is nothing other than the cross
that characterizes the Christian.

Another Work of Mercy

Putting up with annoying people: This too is a work of mercy, and we don't always recognize it as such.

Living side by side, we Christians certainly try to love one another according to Jesus' example and commandment. But despite everyone's good will, occasionally people with very different personalities end up living together. Thus it is comforting to know that to put up with others is a work of mercy: to endure their behavior, their awkward manner, their nagging; basically to lovingly disregard what are really minor shortcomings. Similar to feeding the hungry and visiting the sick, this is one of the works that will be asked of us at our final examination.

With Greater Transparency

Sometimes, especially after a day in which we have sincerely tried to love our neighbor for Jesus, it happens that we feel a special attraction for God. We should, I think, give neither too much nor too little importance to these moments. Certainly, if God feels loved, he draws us to himself.

Initially, we are drawn to him just as we are, with our humanity only partially penetrated by him. We sense these as divine moments, beautiful and pure, because they are directed toward God. But at the same time they are a little heavy because our ego is mixed in.

Then, as we gradually respond to grace, loving God with our actions, conscious of the words, "None of those who cry out 'Lord, Lord,' will enter the kingdom of heaven, but only the one who does the will of my Father in heaven" (Mt 7:21), we begin to feel that our love, which should not be angelic but human-divine, is becoming similar to the heart of Jesus, where all is light and most pure. It is God who loves in us with greater transparency.

Reaching Out. . .

By nature we are not inclined to reach out to those who are suffering, to the poor, to prisoners, to sinners. To do so rather takes a supernatural drive. We should be able to say with Jesus, "People who are in good health do not need a doctor; sick people do. . . . I have come to call, not the self-righteous, but sinners" (Mt 9:12-13).

* * *

Those who assist the sick should be like angels whose efforts go unnoticed, but who are missed when they are not around. This is the trait of love.

When We Receive Communion

At Holy Communion we experience that you love us personally. You give all of yourself to each one of us. Thus, your example of love shatters one of our common illusions. We think that to serve you means to organize great works. Meanwhile we forget to serve you in those we meet every day, as if these encounters had no connection with our life in communion with you.

Mutual Love,

a

Christian Trademark

If You Have Love
for One Another

Once in a while, Lord, it happens that in the midst of the vain hustle through the city streets, amidst the rush, the superficiality, the sadness, there appears in the crowd the ruffling of a Sister's habit. Like an angel, it is a Little Sister of Jesus, who passes by. Her stark simplicity reminds us of the ideal of her founder, Charles de Foucauld, who "cried out" the gospel message with his life. Thus, we too find in our hearts a renewed desire to give witness to you through our own lives, to cry out who you are. . . .

But how can we do the same, "give you" to the world as we pass through the streets, if we live and dress like everyone else, not unlike Jesus and Mary in their times? How can people recognize you through us?

From our heart rises the answer the gospel offers, the solution that you yourself give us: "By this will everyone know that you are my disciples, if you have love for one another" (Jn 13:35). So this is the attire of ordinary Christians — young or old, man or woman, married or single, child or adult, weak or strong. Through their lives they can cry out always and everywhere, the One in whom they believe, the One they want to love.

A Blank Check

B y the very fact that we are Christians, all of us are called to sign a blank check in favor of our neighbor, a check that has the value of our lives. Jesus in fact says, "Love one another even as I have loved you" (Jn 13:34). We know well how he has loved us and with what measure . . .

* * *

T he equilibrium of Christian love lies in loving the person close to us. Thus, starting from our little corner of the world, we will work for the whole of the Church and for all of humanity.

Not Because of Ecstasy

We remember the first Christians not so much because of their ecstasies but because they loved one another. They had grasped the essence of the testament of Jesus, which was still fresh in their minds.

* * *

Nothing is small if it is done out of love.

The Joys and Sufferings
of Others

A mother, bound to her children by a natural love, rejoices in their well-being and shares their every anxiety and concern. How much more should we, united as brothers and sisters by a spiritual bond, consider the joys and the sufferings of others as our own. It is a matter of reviving our faith by living authentic Christian love. This frees us from envy, jealousy, criticism, unwise judgment, and all the other evils that can turn into hell the precious gift of life.

Our Neighbor

O ne of the most direct roads to God
is our neighbor.

* * *

I t is better to be less perfect while remaining in
unity with our neighbor than to be more perfect
but in disunity. Because perfection does not lie in
ideas or in wisdom, but in love.

* * *

W e have to see one another the way God sees us,
not out to criticize and condemn, but filled
with mercy and ready to help one another.

A Witness for Every Age

Saint Bernard, the famous Cistercian of the twelfth century, said in a well-known sermon, "My entire philosophy consists in knowing that Jesus exists and that he was crucified."

Bernard set out with his first companions to follow the road God had shown him. He chose God alone through the way of the cross. "His life with his brothers," says William of Saint Thierry, "was love . . . and those who saw how they loved one another recognized that God was in them." Many people hurried to see them, attracted by God, who in some way became "visible" through the mutual love of these monks.

Perhaps more than ever the world is awaiting this kind of witness, and God is providing it. Despite what critics of religion normally say, a springtime is emerging in many parts of Christianity, among the followers of the great religions as well, and even among people who do not profess a specific faith.

And this blossoming of love is not happening this time among monks alone, but rather among people from all walks of life, both young and old, and of every nationality. They love each other as Christ has taught. And since it is God who lives among them, it is he who attracts many to himself even today.

Jesus'
Testament

Universal Brotherhood

A bove all else, we must fix our gaze on the one Father of so many children. Next, look at all creatures as children of the one Father. We must extend our thoughts and our hearts' affection always beyond the bounds imposed by merely human life and develop the habit of constantly reaching out to the universal brotherhood in only one Father: God.

. . . Jesus, our model, taught us just two things, which ultimately are one: to be children of only one Father and brothers and sisters to one another.

The Celebration

Notwithstanding lofty aspirations and authentic values, we see that people generally yearn for something that fulfills them, that makes them happy. Oftentimes, at any cost. Surely no one desires suffering, and when it comes it is accepted reluctantly since there is no other choice. People of faith might see in it God's will and resign themselves to it. But what people are really looking for is happiness. . . .

Recognizing this irrepressible need, there are those who without scruple produce and sell all kinds of goods to satisfy it. Unfortunately, however, mixed in with the healthy goods and the neutral at most, there are the harmful, even perverted and scandalous goods. Television programs, magazines, and fashion are affected. Often people take in all that is offered, only to realize later, with great disappointment, that they have not found the happiness they were looking for.

Nonetheless, this aspiration to be happy is something positive, because it has been placed into the human heart by God, who is total beatitude.

We too would like to offer people happiness, to "make the world smile." But how can we do this?

If we relieve our neighbors of the burdens that are weighing them down by loving them, by making them feel our love, we help them to be open to wider and brighter horizons. It is not enough to love by carrying out works of mercy, however. Something more is needed.

We have often spoken about unity, and we have affirmed that we can live it only if we are open to receiving it as a grace by living out mutual love. Let us take a deeper look at this grace and analyze it more closely. What, or better who, is unity? Unity is not simply a key-point of our spirituality. Unity brings among us a person, a person who is God himself. Unity is Jesus present among us. Origen says that unity is an "agreement" among people in thought and in sentiment to the point of being of a concord that "associates and contains the Son of God." And we can bear witness to the fact that his presence is the source of very profound happiness. Jesus among us is the fullness of joy. He transforms our lives, as well as the lives of all those who live unity, into an ever-lasting celebration.

Why is this so? Another Father of the Church, John Chrysostom, explains it. Speaking of Pentecost, after which the apostles were so full, so overflowing with grace, light and joy that they appeared to be inebriated, he says: "Even though Pentecost day is over, the celebration, nevertheless, has not ended: Whenever we get together, it is a celebration. How do we reach this conclusion? From the very words of Christ who says: 'Wherever two or three are gathered together in my name, there am I in the midst of them'

(Mt 18:20). Therefore, what greater proof of Christ's presence in our midst could you ask than a gathering filled with a spirit of a celebration?" This is the true celebration people are looking for.

We are called to bring about this celebration in the midst of the world, to help the world experience the joy that brings fullness with it. We should do this and teach others to do it as well, because to act in a way that brings Jesus and his joy among us is nothing other than being Church. The Fathers of the Church, in fact, base their explanations of God's presence in the Church on two phrases: "Where two or three are gathered together in my name, there am I in the midst of them" (Mt 18:20), and "I am with you always, until the end of time" (Mt 28:20). Therefore, we really can be Christ in the midst of the world, not just to make it smile, but to help it live an everlasting celebration.

How to begin? I suggest the taking of initiative in loving everyone, beginning now, and teaching everyone to do the same. The response will come more easily, and sometimes — at least among us — almost automatically. Jesus will be in our midst and, with him, true celebration.

Living Cells

If we take a look at our cities, we might get the impression that we are quite far from the realization of a truly Christian society. The world with its vanity seems to dominate. . . .

We would probably call Jesus' testament utopia if we would not realize that he too lived in a world like ours. At the climax of his life he even appeared to be overcome by it, defeated by evil. He who is God had looked upon the many he had created and had loved as himself. He wanted to forge bonds to unite them as children to their Father and as brothers and sisters to one another. He came to bring the family together again: to make all into one. But despite his words, filled with the ardor and truth that burn away the world's fascination with vanity and uncover the longing for the eternal in every person, many people though they had heard did not want to listen. Their eyes remained blind, because their souls were in darkness.

He had come from heaven to earth and could have saved them all with just a glance. But having created them in his image, as *free* persons, he had to leave them the joy of freely accepting his gift.

Jesus looked out at the world just as we do, but he did not doubt. At night he contemplated heaven above and heaven within him: true Being, Everything real. Outside, he met only with nothingness that passes away.

We should do just as he did and remain bound to the Eternal, to the Uncreated which is the root of all that is created. Believe in the final victory of light over darkness. Pass through the world without wishing to dwell on it. Look to heaven, which is also within us, and stay connected to what has being and value. Make ourselves completely one with the Trinity, who dwells in our souls and enlightens them with eternal light. Then our eyes will no longer be blind. We will look at the world and at things, but it will no longer be us looking but Christ. In us, Christ will again see the blind, the dumb, and the crippled to whom he wants to give sight, speech, and movement: people blind to the vision of God inside and outside them, immobile, unaware of the divine will, which from the depths of their hearts spurs them on to eternal movement, to eternal love.

We too will start to see; we will discover in others the same light which shines within us, the ultimate reality that makes us who we are: Christ in us, who also lives in them. Having found him in these brothers and sisters, we unite ourselves to him in them. Thus a cell of Christ's body comes to life, God's divine fire begins to burn, destined to spread and give light. It is God who makes two into one and places himself as a third, as the relation between them: Jesus among them. In this way love circulates and sponta- neously carries with it, like a river flooding over, everything the two own, both their spiritual and their material goods. To the outside world, this is an effective witness of true, unifying love.

We need of course the courage not to count too much on other means if we want to revive Christianity a bit. We are called to make God live in us and let him overflow unto others, like a stream of life reviving the lifeless, and keep him alive among us by loving one another.

Thus we will see a profound change in all spheres of society that surround us: in politics and art, education and work, private life and entertainment, in everything. Christ is the perfect man, who unites in himself all human beings. Whoever finds him finds the answer to every question.

Christianity for Today

Many people today feel a longing for freedom, for self-affirmation, for community, participation, dialogue, and authenticity. This is why we need to live our Christian ideal fully, since it contains all these aspirations and more.

The truth that is Christ (cf. Jn 14:6) really sets us free (cf. Jn 8:32) from things and from ourselves. If we are deeply united, our individual personality can fully develop its own characteristic; we become new persons (cf. Eph 4:24). If we have Christ among us (cf. Mt 18:20), we are a most exemplary community: a living cell of his body, the Church. Participation is guaranteed, because unity does not exist without complete love for all, without mutual self-giving. We become able to initiate a constructive dialogue, modeled to some extent on the life of the Holy Trinity, where the divine Persons are eternally one and in loving dialogue. We will also be authentic, because truth purifies our old self; it is no longer we who live but Christ in us (cf. Gal 2:20), our true self.

The Art of Giving

There is a special miracle that the gospel message urges us to perform, and that is to share with our brothers and sisters the spiritual riches we may possess. Like Mary, who even gave her own son Jesus, we too need to learn how to give.

We need to give. But this does not imply squandering our goods, which will leave us empty as we may often feel. Rather, we must know how to give with a love that, contrary to emptying our soul, enriches it even more through the new act of love we perform. But how does this work?

In giving we must remain in communion with Jesus: Jesus within ourselves when it is God's will, and in our brothers and sisters in whom we see and love Christ. In this way, we are in communion with Jesus within us and among us, and so there is no danger of giving "holy things to dogs" (Mt 7:6).

This is how Mary lived. This is the life of the Holy Trinity, wherein the second Person remains indissolubly united to the Father and the Holy Spirit, while he was also given to us through the incarnation.

If we live in this way, always in this way, we will pass from richness to richness and we will be perfect as our heavenly Father is perfect (cf. Mt 5:48). Keeping our spiritual treasures for ourselves, instead, will surely dry up our soul, and impede its journey.

If a Neighbor
Has Something Against You

"If you are offering your gift at the altar, and there you remember that your brother has something against you, leave your gift there before the altar and go; first be reconciled to your brother and then come and offer your gift" (Mt 5:23-24).

Divine worship and love among the faithful, which establishes and rebuilds unity, are absolutely inseparable. A community that is not in Christ and fully united cannot worship in a way worthy of the gospel. The Second Vatican Council has reawakened in us the sense of community, the need to be united. In various ways, the Holy Spirit has helped us to rediscover the gospel as a message of love. And how necessary this was! This was why we often lacked a full understanding of the value of the liturgy. For the most part we had inherited an individual religiosity, not overly concerned with mutual love in the community. Although we retained a certain appreciation of the mystery of the liturgy, much had been reduced to form without substance, causing incomprehension and a sense of emptiness. This happens because Christianity often lacks its true strength, love.

What richness of liturgical experience we could expect from a people truly united to God! The Church would shine in all its splendor, attracting many, just as Jesus did in his time.

Christians in Politics

Today, one of the tools that Satan makes use of is political power, but it could be used to serve God. For this to be so, many would need to take up politics as their cross and not hesitate for fear of getting their hands dirty.

Throughout the world, many Christians are engaged in politics, but they are lacking a bond that would make them recognize each other, and be recognized, as brothers and sisters. This bond is Jesus living in their midst (cf. Mt 18:20). His presence would turn them into a powerful force at his service in the world.

We consider missionaries in Thailand or in South America our brothers and sisters, and we desire to help them. But if a Christian is active in another country's political scene, perhaps working hard to pass a Christian law, we do not as readily identify with him or her.

We should bring more faith into politics, more of the mystical into the practical, more wisdom into government, more unity among all.

A Divine Word

Unity: a divine word. If this word were uttered by God Almighty, and people lived it and applied it in every possible way, we would see the world come to a sudden stop and start moving in a different direction. Many would leave the wide path that leads to perdition and choose the narrow one to God. Families divided by quarrels, by lack of understanding and even hatred would be reunited. Children would grow up in an atmosphere of human and divine love, as new people for a Christian future.

Factories, where people are often bogged down by their jobs and where the environment can be rough and depressing, would become places of peace where everyone would do their job for the good of all.

Schools would not limit themselves to transmitting secular knowledge but would transform learning into a stepping stone for reflecting on lasting things. Students would thus develop a sense for the eternal to which our earthly laws and principles point.

Governments would become meeting places for people whose goal would not be their own interest but the common good, including that of other countries.

In other words, the world would become a better place and heaven would touch the earth. Creation would be a harmonious background for all people living in peace.

Is this a dream?
It may seem like one,
and yet, Jesus,
you asked for nothing less than this
when you prayed,
"Your kingdom come,
your will be done
on earth as it is in heaven" (Mt 6:10).

The Root
of the Tree

Suffering Makes Us See

The cross, especially one of prolonged suffering, is one of the greatest gifts that God can send us. Immersed in that suffering, as though transported into the darkness above the atmosphere, our vision of the vast universe is made clearer. When the cross is lacking instead, we may easily mistake lightning bugs for stars. We might think that all we do is in God's service, compatible with and even useful for his glory, but all the while we cater to our own ego and vanity. As a result, we offer God a life that mixes smoke with incense. When, on the other hand, suffering comes to visit us and stays for a long time, we might understand the saints' words that speak of a life away from the limelight, of self-denial and of authenticity before God and our fellow human beings. Such a realization can be so strong as to even cause one to offer acts of gratitude to the One who permits suffering.

The cross certainly brings us to the right path and is the guarantee that the roots of our life are expanding: the sign of new beauty to blossom. And we start to realize that the beatitudes are not merely promises or encouragements but a reality. One who weeps can really find blessing in this very weeping. It is a true beatitude, though not yet the one to come in eternity.

A Mysterious Task

In our daily duties there are always burdensome elements which entail some measure of fatigue and discomfort. But these are the very things that we should appreciate as precious gifts that we can offer to God.

Everything that tastes of suffering is, in fact, of utmost importance. The world does not accept suffering, because it is no longer familiar with the value Christian life gives it, and because suffering goes against our human nature. Thus, the world tries to avoid and to ignore it.

Yet, suffering has a mysterious task: It can become a way to happiness, to that true and enduring happiness which alone can fill our hearts. It is the same happiness that God enjoys and that we humans, destined to what is absolute, can share already in this life.

Precisely through his suffering, Jesus has given joy to every person: joy here on earth and unending joy in the next life. In the same way, by accepting and offering to him our daily worries and concerns, we obtain happiness for ourselves and for others.

The Price We Had to Pay

Sometimes we stop at the crosses
that day by day you have in store for us.
We moan and squirm
like a goat caught in a bramble bush.
We blame this or that,
dream up a thousand reasons,
and invent anything possible
to free ourselves from the bare and harsh beams
    of the cross.

But then there appears on the horizon
a new and radiant dawn,
and we gather the fragrant fruits
which you have brought to maturity
in spite of our imperfect behavior.
In the face of such miracles of your divine love,
we understand the deepest meaning of suffering:
It is the price that we had to pay.

To Suffer for Him

The width of a tree's foliage often corresponds to that of its roots. Similarly, Christ's love expands our hearts through the measure of the pain we have suffered for and offered to him.

* * *

A car goes as long as its fuel lasts. A work of God grows according to the amount of suffering that is transformed into love.

* * *

If we eliminate the cross from our homes, we remove God's blessing from us.

* * *

We can only be fathers and mothers of souls if we are nailed to the cross.

We reach the fire of love only by passing through the ice of suffering.

* * *

Lord, I thank you for the existence of suffering.
Had you not permitted it,
we could not have followed you,
nor would we know the deep joy
of personal union with you.

A Shower of Graces

If I close myself up in sorrow,
I end up contemplating my own misery.
But when I remember that on that night
    you too were overcome by fear,
and when I pour my own drop of sorrow
    into your heart,
then I realize that all of this serves to open wide
    my heart to all of humanity
and to shower the world with your graces.

Seeing Further

S ome men and women have become saints without drawing from particular knowledge, not even religious instruction. They only read from one "book": Jesus crucified. How can we explain this? It must be that they have not merely thought about him, venerated him, or kissed his wounds but have desired to relive him in their own lives.

Whoever suffers and is in darkness sees further than one who is not suffering. The sun has to set before we see the stars.

Suffering teaches what cannot be learned in any other way. It holds the highest chair, the teacher of wisdom. And whoever has wisdom is blessed (Prv 3:13). "Blessed are those who suffer, for they shall be comforted" (Mt 5:4) — not only with their reward in the next life but also with the contemplation of heavenly things here on earth.

We should approach those who suffer with the same and even more reverence with which we used to approach our elders, sure that from them we would receive great wisdom.

Yes to the Cross

To love the cross. It is the only thing we must remember. To love the cross means to dominate all our faculties and keep them on the ray of God's will: to tame them should they refuse, prevent them from going astray, constrain them should they want to escape. Without love for the cross, there is no true love for God or neighbor in our heart.

In Opposition

I read in Matthew's gospel, "Blessed are those who mourn for they shall be comforted" (Mt 5:4). They are striking words. The gospel, then, is in complete opposition to a worldly mentality that looks for all kinds of comfort and well-being, avoiding suffering. Poverty. Mercy toward others. Meekness. Aren't these beatitudes which we are supposed to experience?

If what the gospel tells us here is true, then we should not look at the cross as only a period of life we must go through and be sealed by. The Christian who has chosen God — a crucified God whom he looks out for, loves, and always awaits — should rather expect the cross. The one who has the experience of being "comforted" knows that this is a gift, the result of what the gospel has promised, and not something sought after.

Who Saw More?

The resurrection! John and Peter go to the empty tomb and find the linen cloths on the ground, the shroud on one side (cf. Jn 20:3ff). Mary Magdalene stops and weeps. She sees two angels, one at the head and one at the feet of where Jesus' body had lain. She speaks to them and then, turning, she sees Jesus (cf. Jn 20:12ff).

The apostles didn't see Jesus, even though among them was the one that Jesus loved in a special way, no doubt also because of his innocence. Instead, Mary, the sinner, saw the angels and Jesus.

"Blessed are the pure in heart, for they shall see God" (Mt 5:8). Who saw more on that day? Mary Magdalene. The tears which flowed from her eyes and her vigil outside the tomb — signs of a love which believes and hopes everything; her conversation with the angels and with the person she thought to be the gardener, as though she were the only one concerned about what happened to Jesus; maybe all of this had purified her heart more than the hearts of the others, and so she was privileged to actually see the angels and the Lord.

From this episode, we understand the meaning of the resurrection: Redemption is completed, death conquered, sin overthrown by the stream of mercy that comes from the cross.

God's Word
Evangelizes

Re-Evangelizing Ourselves

When Jesus taught, he spoke with authority. His teachings are the words of the one who is Truth in person. That is why we should assimilate his words anew: Let us take them in one by one, to the point where they penetrate our very being, become part of us, and change our way of thinking, making "new" persons of us.

This is the most profound, deeply-rooted, and effective change necessary for our world today.

Nourished By the Word

God's word," says Pope Paul VI, "is one of his ways to be present among us." Through our sharing of the word, Christ is made present in our souls. In interpersonal relationships verbal communication is quite normal. But when it is God's word that is communicated, something sublime and mysterious happens: Through these words "the divine thought, the Word, the Son of God made man is made known."

When in worrisome and painful moments I have nourished myself with the word of God, my soul has felt fulfilled. And then I realized that this communion with Jesus through his word is possible at all times, and therefore I can *always* be nourished on him. This experience filled me with joy. The gospel is in fact not only a book of consolations to take refuge in and seek answers from in moments of suffering. It has something to say for *every* circumstance; it contains the basic laws of life. Jesus' words are not just to be read but *consumed* by the soul, and thus they make us in every moment similar to him.

When this happens, life's daily events (sufferings or joys, ordinary or extraordinary things) lose their rank of importance or even fall into oblivion, while what really matters is only Christ, who with his word fills them and brings them to life.

The Outfit of Christians

The Word of God is like a set of clothing that outwardly distinguishes Christians, showing the gospel reality of being children of God. The Word protects the fire that grace and love have kindled within us, and keeps it alight. It preserves us from opposing forces that are active in the world and even within our own selves. But above all, the Word of God moves us away from an attitude of defensiveness to one that is active and wins others over.

New People

We can hope for a truly renewed society only if people are renewed by the spirit of the gospel. Wherever they may live or work, they will then live out their faith as they carry out their daily duties. As a result, all existing and valid social structures will acquire new value, while inefficient ones will disappear and be replaced by new ones.

Like a Butterfly Emerging

L ord, we realize that we have many faults.
  But we also rejoice in the certainty
that when we fully live your Word
our imperfections are removed.
We are freed and renewed in every moment,
like a butterfly emerging from its cocoon.
Living your Word means to be another,
to act the part of Another who lives within us.
It means finding our true freedom
by being liberated from ourselves, our faults,
    and our ego.

The Light of the Gospel

From time to time, the light of the gospel reappears in the Church. God seems to awaken minds and hearts so as to revitalize and energize Christianity. While remaining in its essence what it always was, Christianity appears renewed and suited to the needs and demands of the times. This is a clear sign that God is at work in the world and in history.

Imprint of Eternal Life

A t times our lives, in constant thirst for new things, remain flat and spent, saturated in news reports that one moment stimulate and the next moment disappoint.

If we would nourish ourselves more frequently on the eternal words of God — words of wisdom which have overcome the world — we would experience a bath of healing water. We would emerge happier and more fulfilled, because of the mark of immortality printed in our souls.

There Is Another World

"The One who comes from above is above all; the one who is of the earth is earthly, and he speaks on an earthly plane" (Jn 3:31).

This is the difference between Jesus and us: He comes from on high. . . . Jesus brings heaven to us on earth, and he speaks about what he has seen and heard. Besides the one we know, there is another world, the one from which Jesus came, where you truly see and hear.

We come from the earth. That is why what we say and what he "who comes from heaven" says is different. His words are *eternal.*

A life spent intelligently is the one which translates the gospel message into daily life, and whose supreme ideal is to incarnate the words of heaven.

The Love
of a Mother

A Lay Person Like Us

Today much is said about the role of the laity. Perhaps the image of the lay person, who after all is "Church" as well, would become clearer if we would think about Mary. Certainly, Mary's calling is unique. Nonetheless, I believe that she could be the role model of every lay person.

Catholics do not make a god out of Mary as some have suggested, yet we still distance her to a sphere of her own; but neither is this her rightful place. Love and faith have led us to discover all that is extraordinary about her. We praise her as Mother of God, Immaculate, Assumed into Heaven, and Queen, but not as the perfect Christian, as fiancee, bride, mother, widow, virgin, role model of every Christian. Like us who are lay persons, she cannot offer Christ to the world sacramentally, for she is not part of the Church's hierarchy. Yet she is active in the Church, as a mother who, prompted by the love in her heart, shares through her own sacrifice in the sacrifice of her Son.

Mary, lay person like us, reminds us that the essence of Christianity is love, that even a priest or bishop must first of all be a true Christian: ready to love as Jesus did when on the cross he founded his Church.

Highlighting in the Church what is fundamental in love, that is, the unifying element, Mary presents to the world the Church, the Bride of Christ, as Jesus wanted her to be and as people today expect her to be: a community ordered by love. Only if the Church highlights this fundamental aspect can she enter into a fruitful dialogue with the world. While often less open to the hierarchy, people are responsive to the witness of love given by the Church, which is the soul of the world.

Like an Open Book

A mother does not stop loving her children if they go off track. When they stray, she waits for their return. Her only desire is to have them near again, to forgive them, to embrace them once more. The love of a mother is full of mercy. The love of a mother always goes beyond whatever painful situation her child may be in. It never falters even in the face of moral, ideological or other storms her child might end up in. Her love goes beyond everything, ready to cover it all, to keep it hidden. If a mother sees her own child in danger, she does not hesitate to risk everything, even her own life if necessary. . . . The love of a mother is stronger than death. . . .

If such is the love of ordinary mothers, imagine Mary, mother of God, mother of Jesus and — in a spiritual sense — mother of us all! She is *the* mother, the model of motherhood, of motherly human love. And since God is love, she opens up to us the mystery of God, like an open book that explains God to us. God's love was so great that his Son died the harshest of deaths on the cross. And this for us, in order to save us, just like a mother who would do anything for her child. Mary, mother of God, is the created being that more than anyone else mirrors and shows God to us.

Let us revive our faith in Mary's love for us, trust in her love, and imitate her. She can be a role model for every Christian. She shows us the most direct way to God.

Giving Up God's Gift

Mary Desolate! We may think that we have given up everything, that we are not unduly attached to anything. But there may be something that we believe we *can* possess and must show to others, and we enjoy doing so: I am thinking of the gifts that God has given us.

If in her desolation Mary sacrificed God for God, we too must know how to lose God's gifts for God. So let us not linger over them, not admire them in a way that would fill our souls with spiritual pride. If our souls are free, they can be filled with God's Spirit.

If we do possess gifts, they are given to us so that we may use them well, with a love which must animate everything we do. But it is important not to dwell on them, to be detached from them, so as to be only love: love for others and love for the works of the Church. Love thinks only about the beloved, not about itself.

The Way to Jesus

No one more than Mary, Jesus' mother and ours, points us the way to him. Therefore, we would like to show her our love in many different ways, but above all we should do so by imitating her in her desolation.

If we walk in Mary's company, our path will be more smooth and less marked by those upheavals and inner tribulations which are unavoidable without her. If we live with Mary, so the saints tell us, even our worst enemy, the Evil One, will be put to flight. Furthermore, with her we will avoid the danger and havoc of spiritual pride. Where Mary is present, there is true humility.

Mary was present at our baptism, the beginning of our life as Christians. At every new spiritual stage she is still present, as teacher and mediator of those graces. And at the end of our lives, she will be there waiting to open heaven for us and take us to Jesus.

In every moment of my life, may I lose everything but Mary, Mary Desolate.

Letting Go of Ourselves

At times a worry may pass through our mind: How am I faring in God's eyes? Does anything cloud my limpid relationship with him? Even should we consider ourselves perfect, still how small must we be in front of God who is ultimate perfection!

But how can we know the state of our affairs? The best thing, I believe, is not to analyze, not to think of ourselves at all, but rather look to God alone, to his will, and to Jesus who is present in our brothers and sisters. We must be "outside of ourselves," not looking for our own holiness but for the One who is holy. This is where love and true holiness lies.

As in all other cases, even here we must remember that Mary Desolate lost everything, including her own self. Taken only by God, who fills such a deep abyss, she is the teacher also in this work of "forgetting" ourselves, and of living in God.

Once in a while I have a sense of feeling lost, of not being anchored to anything firm; a feeling that circumstances govern my life which, yes, is lived in God's service, but without the certainty of belonging totally to him. This causes me pain, and I feel like a person drifting on a rough sea.

I am looking for you, my God, for a way to possess you alone and not let my ego be in your way, this ego which is so annoying and from which there seems to be no escape.

In those moments, I remember a discovery that gave me the certainty of being able to reach holiness: I think of Mary under the cross and take her as a model in my efforts to reach Christian perfection. Thus, more than ever determined to carry on God's work, I want to follow this ideal of life, not lose my way, but safely reach the harbor.

Powerlessly under the Cross

L oving Mary and becoming similar to her can mean many things. She stood under the cross and lost her Son (cf. Jn 19:25ff). Sometimes we too need to lose all we have in Jesus, only to find it again at the right time, multiplied and developed. What happened to Mary might happen to us in a similar way: Standing at the foot of someone's cross, unable to remove from that person either the interior, spiritual or the exterior, physical pain, which might bring him or her to the brink of despair. We would prefer to take that person's place ourselves. But instead we need to assist inactively and powerlessly as "the grain of wheat dies," and all we have is the hope that it will germinate and bear fruit (cf. Jn 12:24f).

For now, we can only contribute our suffering, not even able to comfort the person we love, but rather send to heaven our plea of mercy for both of us who, each in our own way, are giving our lives.

> Standing powerlessly under the cross. . . .
> Mary, you are our mother and know us.
> You know such sufferings.
> Relieve those who suffer,
> Shorten their time,
> And hasten the hour of relief.

Certainty of Holiness

Mary under the cross tells me what holiness really means. I want to re-live her self-denial, belong to God alone. Even when I am among people, my life should be an intimate dialogue with God. That is why I want to put aside my words, thoughts and deeds until God's time for them has come.

Mary under the cross gives us the certainty of holiness. She is a perennial source of union with God, a fountain of overflowing joy.

Mary under the cross is my discovery. In her I have found my way.

Stabat Mater

S tabat Mater. . ." What heroic virtues shine in
Mary as she stood on Calvary at the foot of the
cross (cf. Jn 19:25).

What a mother! To have a son who is God himself,
and to see him die in that way! And she lived through
it! Only her being the *mother of God* explains to us how
she could find that strength.

There we were born to new life, there we were
made children of God through Christ (cf. Gal 4:4f),
and when Jesus handed her over to John, we became
children of Mary. But what did the birth of the
Church, the Spouse of Christ, cost her? Christ
himself. Here we understand how the Church is truly
the mystical body of Christ.

> Mary, you have loved us so much!
> Give us just a little of your faith,
> a little of your hope and your love,
> your strength and perseverance,
> your humility and purity,
> your meekness and your mercy,
> all your virtues.
>
> As often as we think of them,
> we understand how much you lived them.

Jesus entrusted the Church to you.
We dare to ask you that the Church,
which we have so much at heart,
may soon be united.
God's grace makes you all-powerful!
You can do it.

The Life

of

the Church

A Passion for the Church

Christians should be filled with a "passionate love for the Church" (Paul VI). A love that should not only be felt but also practiced and extended to the entire Church. And this includes all its institutions, fruit of so many charisms that the Holy Spirit has given and continues to give to the Church. This love leads to a more profound understanding of the Church, and understanding, in turn, leads to deeper love.

What is true for interpersonal relationships should also hold true among groups. On a personal level we Christians are called to love, to get to know one another, to make ourselves one with others, and to share with them the gifts God has given us. Similarly, we should get to know, esteem, and love other movements and associations in the Church, fostering a sharing of our spiritual patrimonies. From this a collaboration might result which would truly help us to serve with our hearts and minds the Church we love. Otherwise, our love for the Church would be purely rhetorical, and we would run the risk of being closed and isolated.

Even the love we nurture for the pope cannot go beyond the level of feeling and superficial enthusiasm if we do not share the concern for what he loves the most: the life of God's *entire* Church.

The Mosaic

Take a moment and imagine a mosaic. There are beautiful ones in the Roman basilicas. . . . Also in the Near East there are many; I remember some in the Basilica of Our Savior in Istanbul. What splendor: dazzling centuries-old gold, magnificent sky-blue backgrounds, landscapes . . . and those royal thrones upon which Jesus is seated! What art, what beauty and majesty!

Mosaics, as we know, are made of many small tiles or stones. The Church too can be compared to a mosaic, and in it each one of us can be considered a tile. But the tiles of this mosaic are not inanimate. In the mosaic that is the Church, each one of us is a *living* tile. We understand where we fit in and are aware of our specific role in relation to everyone else and to the whole. While we know that each of us has value only as part of the whole, we are also aware that if one of us is missing the mosaic is incomplete.

Not all the tiles of this mosaic are the same, of course. One of us, so to speak, might be a green tile, another a blue one, still another a golden or white one, and so on. That is, we all have a specific task to be carried out right where we are, an individual mission to remain faithful to. Thus, as tiles in the Church's mosaic, we must remain in the place assigned to us.

Carrying out our specific duty, we give of ourselves, and this is also the best way to find true communion with our neighbors. We love them and, since they too live for others, they love us in return. Just like in a living body, this reciprocal giving and receiving increases the unity in the splendid mosaic that is the Church.

Such is the nature of the Church, and we need to keep it in mind. Imagine, for example, a mosaic with the image of a young man. Someone might say, "Look at his beautiful and vivid eyes. Are they not the most beautiful part? I want to be the eye!" If others would say the same, imagine what kind of mosaic we would have. It would be disfigured and incomprehensible.

So let us remember that we are living tiles of the Church, all linked to one another, and each one participating in the whole. If a particular tile is missing, everyone lacks something, and all suffer the consequences. So we all need to accomplish our task faithfully, which means doing God's will moment by moment.

Personal Apostolic Involvement

With evil on the rise in many places — factories, schools, neighborhoods — we cannot limit ourselves to being just "practicing Christians." Going to church on Sunday, having a good family, and being honest at work is not enough. Our times demand personal apostolic involvement, so as to safeguard and reinforce Christianity, and lead others to God. In the face of those attempting to remove God from the world, we need to give the world back to God and God back to the world.

Love in the Church

John Paul II has declared Therese of Lisieux a doctor of the Church. . . . In his address, he highlighted her discovery which can be encapsulated in her own words, "In the Church, my mother, I will be love."

She longed to have many vocations in the Church, among others, to the priesthood and to the missions. But God's will for her was different, and through the Holy Spirit she understood her specific task: to "be love." To be love, however, did not simply remain a discovery for Therese; it became her very life. Her brief life was marked by an admirable and boundless trust in God and was filled with continuous acts of love, not only for God, but also for her neighbor. Therese had found her place in the Church.

To be love in the Church, however, is not Therese's vocation alone. It is the most imminent calling of every Christian woman today. And with Therese, women are newly convinced that what gives meaning to their lives is precisely love. And this gives origin to what the pope calls the "genius of woman."

Thus, Therese's discovery brings into light a principle in the Church that men and women of our times are called to live out: The Marian principle or profile, whose model is Mary, and to which everybody is called. Perhaps also because Therese highlights this particular aspect of Christian life and doctrine, she was recognized a doctor of the Church. Love, which the Holy Spirit has poured into our hearts, makes us participate in the life of God.

Therese's thoughts and reflections on love as the essence of every other Christian vocation, call to mind an exquisite passage which Patriarch Athenagoras used to tell me and which concerned the Holy Spirit: "Without the Holy Spirit, God is distant, Christ remains in the past, the gospel is a dead letter, the Church a mere organization, authority is domination, mission a kind of propaganda, and our actions a moral code for slaves. But with the Holy Spirit, Christ the risen Lord becomes present, the gospel a source of life, the Church trinitarian communion, authority a liberating service, mission a Pentecost, liturgy a commemorative celebration and anticipation, our actions become divine." Without the love the Spirit pours forth, everything loses meaning.

This is what Therese of the Child Jesus, doctor of the Church, knew, and this is what she can teach us.

Our Calling

The Gospel of John says: "Any who did accept him he empowered to become children of God. These are they who believe in his name — who were begotten not by blood, nor by carnal desire, nor by man's willing it, but by God" (Jn 1:12-13).

Perhaps we do not think enough about our Christian calling. Perhaps we too live as if begotten "by carnal desire," by human will, and do not give enough witness to what it means to be a child of God. Perhaps we do not fully understand the consequence of having met during our lifetime the Word become flesh and of having believed. It is this believing in him that makes us children of God.

How thankful we can be for such a calling! And what a responsibility we have to share this message of salvation with others.

Holiness Becomes Visible

It doesn't happen every day to meet saintly persons. But when it does, holiness becomes visible, in their recollection during prayer or at Mass, and even in their way of just moving about. As with love and compassion they share the joys and sorrows unique to those they meet, what shines in their faces could only be divine.

God
Pure Spirit

God Alone

Holy Spirit,
we ask you for nothing but God alone.
Soon, maybe in ten or twenty years,
we shall come to you
to adore you in your kingdom
where you reign and all things exist for you alone.
Therefore, we implore you:
Grant us that in the time that remains
we may live only for you.
Because you alone we wish to love,
and you alone we want to serve.

God, pure spirit
to whom we can offer our human nature
like an empty chalice for you to fill.
May you shine
from our heart and our being,
from our face and our words,
from our action and our silence,
from our living and our dying,
for as long as we live in this world
and even after we have left.
Wherever possible,
may we leave behind
the luminous trail of God's presence:

Traces of him present in us,
amidst the world's structures and ruins;
a world alive or falling
in the midst of the glory or the vanity of all things;
all a footstool or pushed aside
to make room for the One
who is all, who is love.

Receptive to the Holy Spirit

O Holy Spirit,
we should be thankful to you so many times,
and yet we thank you so rarely.
Though we are consoled to know
that you are one with Jesus and the Father,
this does not justify us.
We want to be near you. . . .
Greatest consoler,
sweet guest of our soul,
you refresh our lives.
You are Light, Joy, Beauty.
You attract us, inflame our hearts,
and inspire our thoughts.
You help us to live lives committed to holiness.
You accomplish in us
what many sermons would not have taught.
You sanctify us.

Holy Spirit,
you are so gentle
and at the same time strong and overwhelming.
You blow like a light breeze
which few know how to listen to.
Look at our lack of finesse
and make us receptive to your grace.

May no day pass
in which we don't invoke you and thank you,
adore you and love you,
listen to your voice.
This grace we ask from you.
And wrap us in the great light of your love,
especially in our darkest hour,
when the vision of this life will come to a close
and dissolve itself into the next.

A Loving Response

During holy communion, I thought of the heart of Jesus: His heart that I adore in the eucharist and in heaven, where his heart is always in the company of the heart of Mary.

With great joy, I reflected upon the kind of heart with which the glorious Jesus loves us. I was wondering what my response toward the heart of Jesus could be. I had an intuition: Heart calls for a heart. "A heart for a heart," therefore, is my proposal for today and forever, as long as God wants it.

A heart for a heart. This means that I must make my own the reality of "letting go" without half measures, so as to be completely receptive to the Holy Spirit. He alone in me is able to love the heart of Jesus worthily. Thus I need to put aside everything, let go of it all, even the most beautiful and holy things, all that I could legitimately love, but which are not God.

*In
Silence*

Pray Like This

Thy will be done on earth as it is in heaven" (Mt 6:10).
What a great thing you make us ask for, my God!
Alas, in this world, who does your will for real and all
the time? You are the Perfect One, the Absolute One,
and you ask for perfect and absolute things. Is this
not why you have come?

"Give us this day our daily bread" (Mt 6:11).

This day. You really want us to live *your* way, Lord!
But who lives like this, "this day" and only for this
day? Who is ready to abandon themselves to the
future, carefree like the birds whose food and
clothing you provide?

Living only for this day would simplify many
things, but it also makes us worry, since we feel a
natural need to have a secure future. Yet, there may
not be a tomorrow. . . .

You, Lord, want us to be vigilant. For on a day and
at an hour unknown to us you will call us to yourself.
For the time that we still have, help us then to live
each day well.

"And forgive us our debts" (Mt 6:12).

You do not say "sins," you say "debts." Yes,
because sinning means not loving, and love is the one
and only debt which we owe in this life (cf. Rom
13:8).

Adoration

Reading the biography of Saint Peter Eymard, founder of the Blessed Sacrament Fathers, seems like a continuous discovery of the infinite treasures contained in the eucharist. The saint appears immersed in the eucharist as if it would be the heaven of his soul, the cell of his religious life. His is the famous saying, "Our age is ill because it does not practice adoration."

To adore. . . What thirst we ourselves feel for it at times. To kneel, with our heads down to the floor, especially spiritually, before our Creator and Lord, a need for our created souls.

To adore means recognizing our own nothingness before God Almighty and saying: You are everything, you are who you are, and I was given the privilege to live and to recognize this.

Peter Eymard discovered aspects of the spiritual life which the entire Church has since made her own. Pope Pius XI beautifully described his method of prayer: "Peter Eymard gathered up from every age, from the depths of tradition . . . the understanding that the eucharist sublimely summarizes the essence and practice of worship: adoration, thanksgiving, reparation and supplication. This is what religion is, that attitude that every human person can and must have before one's Creator."

Christ's Greatest Desire

I came across a sentence of the gospel that touched me: "Whatever you ask for in prayer . . . believe that you have received it and it will be yours" (Mk 11:24).

In various ways, Jesus spoke of asking: "Knock. . ." (Mt 7:7), "Everything you ask in my name. . ." (Jn 14:13) — words through which we perceive his love. But even stronger is this one where he adds, "believe that you have received it and it will be yours."

Jesus wants us to believe: Even before we have asked for it, we have already obtained the grace. Isn't this a paradox? It shows how much Christ loves us, loves *me*.

But when in difficult and apparently hopeless moments we have asked with that kind of faith and really *have* received, then our trust in his love turned into certainty. And this has happened more than once. . . .

Christ's all-powerful heart, so human and divine, wishes no more perhaps than to share with his brothers and sisters the immense treasures which are his.

In Silence

Occasionally, I have the opportunity to recollect myself in a solitary place and pray. Then I notice how this silence, uninterrupted by telephone, radio, traffic or other noises, speaks to me.

I find that in noisy environments God is silent, but where there is silence he speaks.

It often happens that I may pick up a book to meditate only to put it down again, because God wants to speak within me. And I understand the anchorites, the Carthusians, and the Trappists. I sense how fulfilled their lives can be, how filled with conversations, and in what special company they find themselves.

For me, however, these conversations are only meant to be moments of consolation from God, a help to continue my work. Thus, I newly direct my attention to the humanity I need to serve, so as to carry out the work which God has entrusted to me. This is my way to respond to his love, to the words he silently speaks to me in the depths of my heart.

All I wish and hope for, if only out of his mercy, is to feel called and loved by him.

Water from This Fountain

We often make resolutions, but we don't always manage to keep them.

In some rare instances, however, a certain resolution appears not to come from ourselves; it seems, rather, as if God himself is calling us gently and decisively, and we can't help but keep the resolution.

These are moments we have to thank God for. In them he calls us to real life, to himself who lives within us. There we find peace harmonizing everything, light dispelling every darkness, his presence filling every void.

This can happen at any time. We feel his presence. He is in me and I in him. Two, and yet we are one. Because I am water from this fountain, a flower from this seed, witness of his presence, which fills my being.

This, really, is what living means.

God alone knows how to take form within us. We are only capable of ruining it.

Jesus Knows Everything

Jesus knows everything. He reads our hearts, knows our thoughts.

How consoling to be sure of this, when for example from the bottom of our hearts we ask him for favors or praise him or want to express our love for him. He knows about it; he perceives it all.

Think of the encounter of Thomas and the risen Christ: Jesus knew everything about Thomas. He knew that Thomas wanted to put his finger into the nail marks and his hand into his side. Jesus, who is God, knows everything.

What a comfort for those who pray. God does listen to us, and this is enough for us. Whether or not he then grants our request is not the point; after all, he knows what is good for us.

Thomas replies with the wonderful words, "My Lord and my God!" (Jn 20:28), and these same words also spring from our hearts as we read this gospel passage.

Our
Eternal Destiny

No Longer With Us?

When a friend or a relative of ours leaves for the next life, we usually say they are "no longer with us"; we think of them as being lost. But this is not so. If we reason in this way, where is our faith in the communion of saints?

No one who enters into God can be lost to us. Their lives have changed, but it has not been taken away. Their love, everything of real value in them, remains. Yes, everything else does pass away, even faith and hope, but love remains (cf 1 Cor 8:13). And so does our neighbors' true love for us, since it is rooted in God. After all, God is not so lacking in generosity that he would take away from us what he himself gave us through our neighbor. Rather, he continues to give it, just in another way. Our friends who passed on to the next life continue to love us, and they now do so with a love that is unfaltering.

Let us believe, then, in the love of our brothers and sisters who have reached the goal; let us ask them for graces for us who are still on the journey. For our part, let us pray for our beloved departed, which after all is a work of mercy too.

No, our friends are not lost. They simply left their home to go and live in another place. They now dwell in the heavenly homeland, in God, and through him we can continue to love one another as the gospel has taught us.

Our Meeting With You

L amb of God" (Jn 1:36) is how John the Baptist addresses Jesus. From the start, he sees Jesus as a victim, chosen by God himself.

The same should and indeed needs to apply to each Christian. We are born to be a living offering, to die with Christ, and then to share in his glory. We should look forward to the day of our meeting with him like a bride looks forward to her bridegroom. That hour comes for everyone and, what is more, it comes like a thief, at a time in which we are not expecting it (cf. Lk 12:35ff). It makes sense, therefore, to live each moment in view of that hour, and to act accordingly. Thus, our life will acquire true meaning.

Certainly, it is good and necessary to work for a better world of tomorrow, which is best done by spreading a Christian lifestyle. And this not least in view of our brothers and sisters who are yet to come in the future, because we want to love them too as Christ has taught us. But as far as we ourselves are concerned, we should always be alert, open to the call to enter into the life to come, into the kingdom which is not of this world.

My God,
what a mystery is the life
that you have given us.
And what a trial (death) it has to undergo,
to reach its goal, our eternal home.

Thank you
for having come among us,
and for showing us the way,
for *making yourself* the way.
Lost in you,
we will always live in the light,
even amidst the deepest darkness.

Thank you
for becoming man,
for having lived among us
and having died for us (cf. Rom 5:8), for me.
Yes, died.
Had you not died,
how could we face death?
Now we will think of you,
and die with you,
even in our last moment.

If we were to make Jesus who dies our ideal, we would see an unimaginable flourishing of life for many.

More than Just Resigned

With God's help, I want to be more than just resigned to the fact that one day I need to face my final agony and death. Usually, we look at the ill and the dying as a category apart. We surround them with a special, even supernatural, atmosphere. But shouldn't we try to *always* live as if today were our last day, our last hour?

Before dying Christ said: "Father . . . glorify your Son" (Jn 17:1). In his eyes, it was a beginning therefore, not an ending. And Peter speaks similarly of "the crown of glory" (1 Pt 5:4) awaiting us.

This is Christianity. Therefore, I will accept the sufferings that this day will bring me as stepping stones to the final trial, that is, my final agony and struggle. I will look at them as exercises to develop patience, perseverance, trust in God, and a passion for the cross, which ultimately will carry me to glory.

An Illusion

Without a doubt, we can and should love the world, because everything beautiful is directly or indirectly a work of God. But given that eternity and heaven exist, our short life needs to gain its proper perspective and its true meaning with this in mind.

Our life here on earth is like a test. Our purpose and destiny do not belong to this but to a future day in another world. If we cling more and more to this earth and all it has to offer, if we are only concerned about living in comfort "down" here, then our life is off track, an illusion. In this case, we cannot hope for a future life, and we already know that our present life will come to an end.

Granted, we can go with the times, be people of today. But to avoid a serious mistake, we should first of all be people of eternity, people who already partake in everlasting life, people who follow in the footsteps of the truly wise, the true saints.

Sometimes their austere lifestyle, their mortifications and detachment from the world may baffle us. But their reason is sound. It is all the rest that is false. "Whoever loves his life will lose it, and whoever hates his life in this world will save it" (Mt 16:25).

The Grain of Wheat

God became man and therefore mortal. He was born on this earth to give his life. This, then, is the meaning of life: To live like the grain of wheat, which dies and passes for the true and never-ending life.

We should journey through the world with this attitude toward life: Every day brings us closer to our death where *Life* begins. If we encounter illnesses on the way, we should see them as steps prepared by the love of God to help us scale the heights, as trials to prepare us for *the* trial. We are like small hosts that are not yet completely consumed, awaiting the moment of the *consummatum est* ("it is accomplished"), which will come for all of us. Thus we are mortals with the mortal God-man so as to rise with him to a life that will never end.

Lord,
in suffering, in the "Mass"
for which we prepare,
may our living your will
be our precious gift to you,
which we offer like incense.

Lord,
may we hasten without reluctance
toward the goal of our journey
which is near.
May we give ourselves completely to you
before death comes like a thief to steal us away.
May we offer you
what is most precious to us,
as the Father offered his only-begotten Son,
as Mary offered Jesus,
and all saints their Works.

Then,
when you call us,
nothing will change:
Death will be a splendid
and an almost imperceptible passage
to the next life,
in unity with you, our God,
who in your goodness became flesh
and suffered the agony of the cross
so that you could go before us,
in death and in never-ending life.

Thought of Paradise

If we would think more frequently of the heaven that awaits us in the next world, our faces would less often show sadness. We wouldn't let our moments drag on like people who feel that their lives are just about over anyway.

* * *

Each day passes and evening comes. When will the day come that knows no evening? When that day comes, Lord, may I be worthy to live eternally in your light, which never grows dim.

Longing for Paradise

At times, when we feel the burdens of this life, we are filled with a longing for paradise. But then an inner voice invites us to recollect, to be alone before the Eternal One, to be consoled by him, and to be ready to continue this life for as long as he wishes us to.

In moments like these we feel like a child, who is picked up and taken into its mother's arms — and needs nothing else. Thus we find new strength, and we understand that it would not be good to already go to enjoy the place God's goodness has prepared for us. It would not even be right, since we realize that for such eternal bliss, we must become worthy of it.

Then, like flowers that awake and bloom in the warmth of the spring sun, heroic resolutions are reborn in our heart. We are ready to face our daily challenges with courage and determination and live them to the fullest for the time we have left. Recalling words and thoughts that have given us strength in the past, we choose one of them to take to heart, to be our guide at least for this day.

He Wants to Give Us Everything

> "Father, I want those you have given me to be with me where I am, so that they may always see the glory you have given me because you loved me before the foundation of the world. Father, Righteous One, the world has not known you but I have known you, and these have known that you have sent me. I have made your name known to them and will continue to make it known, so that the love with which you loved me may be in them, and so that I may be in them" (Jn 17:24-26).

Christ wants to give us paradise. He wants us to be where he is, show us his eternal glory.

He invokes the Father, reminds him of his "righteousness," and asks for us — not for the world that has not known him but for us — the very love with which the Father has loved him.

What fathomless mystery! More than ever, in his testament Jesus reveals himself as God.

There seems to be nothing of purely human nature in these trinitarian words. But at the same time we feel the heart of a friend, of a brother, of a loving teacher, of a father who gives to his own *everything* he can: participation in his divinity.

A Heart of Flesh

What will Jesus be like in paradise? He is certainly glorified also as a human being. And Mary, his mother assumed into heaven, is sufficient reward for his life, death and passion through which he preserved her from sin. Yet his involvement with humankind must make him want us too, who are now his brothers and sisters, to ascend to the place he has prepared for us.

What the heart of a God-man desires ultimately cannot be fully understood! But this heart of flesh which, though transfigured, still beats in heaven, must surely be filled with ardor and tenderness, with hope and inexhaustible, never-ending love. But oftentimes we don't fully understand the truth and beauty of our religion, and we venerate the heart of Jesus in a rather naive way. Thus, the world of today with its discoveries and boundless aspirations can no longer understand it. And yet, this heart is like a sun that shines on the whole world and on every human person.

We must believe and trust in this heart, which will never delude us. It is a source of great hope for every human being; a lamp that shines even amidst the dark moments of life.

Spiritual
Fruitfulness

"You Are Gods"

Virginity pleasing to God does not consist so much or only of a specific lifestyle. It is an inner attitude of living not for oneself but wholeheartedly for God. Whoever lives this way is entirely pure and transparent. It is the transparency of Mary, who was never concerned with herself but only with God, with Christ, and with his mystical body, the Church.

Virginity pleasing to God, therefore, is equivalent to love. A love that burns everything like a fire and makes us participate in the life of God, who himself is love and who in his intimate life — which is perfect reciprocal giving — lives divine virginity.

Virgins live their lives not leaning on anyone. They count on God alone, and precisely in this they find their support. Since they trust solely and fully in God, he comes to uphold them and give them strength.

To no one more than to virgins who are serving God's kingdom applies the scripture sentence, "You are gods" (Jn 10:34; Ps 82:6). They are "deified" by taking part, as much as this is possible, in God's life.

Hard to Understand

Something that the world will never understand is the spiritual fruitfulness of virgins given entirely to God. Just as God chose a virgin to become the mother of Christ, so he chooses virgins to prepare the ground for the coming of Christ in people's hearts.

A true virgin is a mother of souls. And in God's eyes, this kind of motherhood is more precious still than the natural one. However, what makes a person virginal is his or her love for God. That is why anyone — mothers and fathers of a family, children, elderly persons, the engaged — can live out a spiritual motherhood or fatherhood. All they need to do is love God, place him first in their lives, and give room to the Holy Spirit, who will give charity its order in them. This opens up great opportunities of growth for the kingdom of God in the world.

Not Alone

A woman wholly given to God and bride of Christ is not alone. She belongs to One who in moments of weakness and uncertainty gives her the inner strength of divine grace.

Still, many in the world think that such a person is alone. They might look at her decision with good will and consider it heroic. But in her heart lives the kingdom of God; she enjoys a communion with the Trinity, who dwells within her. Thus, she too lives in a family that is divine and complete: She and God within her, plus all those who are born or reborn to true life from the faithfulness lived out in this relationship.

Beatitudes
and
Virtues

Taking the Beatitudes Seriously

We need to admit that as Christians we rarely are the way Christ would want us. It would be much different, for example, if we would take the beatitudes seriously.

Rather than falling prey to passivity, we would have the meekness that peacefully wins over the world.

In places of sorrow, we would not find bitter resignation but persons who would continue to thank the Lord, even amidst tears.

People, while living in the midst of the world, would not let themselves be entrapped by its mire, and would look at other persons and the events around them with pure eyes, from God's point of view.

Poverty would not result in spiritual deprivation but be a wellspring for the kingdom of God.

Hatred and vengeance would disappear, since interpersonal relationships would be pervaded by forgiveness and mercy.

But often our world presents an altogether different and melancholic picture: where sorrow brings only sorrow, and those who die are forgotten, even though they now belong to a life that never ends.

The Gospel Lifestyle

Why is it that sometimes we are not fully happy? Why is our joy overshadowed by pain and worry? Not least, probably, because we lack that great virtue of hope.

Even a fleeting glance at the gospels portrays hopeful expectation. The gospels are full of God's promises.

If we want to renew our life as Christians, if we want to break through to the liberating joy of children who live the gospel, we need a hope that perseveres.

Paul calls the Lord, "God, the source of hope." It is so true. The one, true God fills you "with all joy and peace" (Rom 15:13). Joy and peace: Two things the world is lacking and which are gifts Christians can offer.

A True Christian

Nicholas of Flüe was a father of ten, a farmer, soldier, politician, and judge — and in all this a person profoundly united to God. Upon God's wish and in agreement with his wife Dorothy, he withdrew to be a hermit, not far from his estate. Leaving his eldest son to look after his family, for twenty years he lived a life of contemplation and of total fasting. Nevertheless, he became the "father" of his country, Switzerland, saving it at a most critical moment of internal strife. He also acted as adviser to politicians of neighboring countries.

We can only be stunned and amazed at such a life. But what strikes us even more is his reply to a bishop, who had been sent to Nicholas to question him about his fasting. "Which is the greatest virtue, the one most pleasing to the Lord?" asked the bishop. "Obedience," came the reply. Though it took an enormous physical effort, out of obedience he ate a morsel of bread and drank a sip of wine, which caused the bishop to embrace him with affection.

Yes, Nicholas was a true Christian, who lived obedience. And we want to remember this especially in our times.

In the Hour of Success

S aint Margaret of Cortona's confessor related the following story about her: One night, Satan tempted her with the flattering thought that she was well regarded by everyone. In response, she went to the terrace of her house and, weeping, began to shout: "Wake up, people of Cortona! Wake up! I am asking you to wake up, throw stones at me, and drive me away, because I am a sinner. I have committed the following sins against God and my neighbor . . ." And at the top of her lungs, she proceeded to list all her faults. It is a wonderful lesson on humility, on the truth of who we really are.

If in the Church we belong to a Work of God, which may have found approval and is experiencing success, let us make sure that we distinguish between ourselves and this Work, between ourselves and what God is accomplishing through us. Otherwise, the Evil One may use our arrogance and pride and lead us, like thieves, to appropriate to ourselves what belongs to God. That is why we want to repeat with Augustine, "Lord, may I know *myself*, and may I know *you*."

True humility does not mean saying that we have not accomplished anything. It is a matter of attributing to God what is his and to ourselves what is ours.

Living Humility

There is something about humility that attracts us. It shows us who we are and who God is. We, by ourselves, are nothing. We would live humility well if we learn how to accept this nothingness that we are and the everything that God is. The best way to accomplish this is to live the divine will in the present moment. This is when we have humility.

The aspiration of every human person is to be God. John of the Cross says, "What God wants is to make us gods by participation, he being God by nature." God by participation; Being by participation. I would wish to be Being, so that Being could in every moment speak to the world of himself. But this can happen if I am free of myself, of my own will and thoughts.

Mary must have been like this.

What Matters Is the "How"

On a human plane, some days go better than others. And so, once again we experience that in the present moment given to us, it doesn't really matter if the day is going well or not. What does matter instead is *how* we live our lives, a *how* that points to love, which alone gives value to everything. God, in fact loves those who keep his word.

Let us keep in mind that neither our successes nor our failures will accompany us to the next life. Were we to even give our bodies to be burned — without love it would have no meaning. Without love neither doing missionary work nor speaking with angels' tongues, neither doing works of mercy nor giving everything to the poor has value (cf. 1 Cor 13:1ff).

We can take with us to heaven only how all this was lived, that is, in accordance with God's word through which our love is expressed.

Let us start our day then with confidence, whether there be storms or sunshine. Let us remember that every day has value insofar as we have assimilated the word within us. Christ will live in us, and he will give value to the works we accomplish, whether directly or through our prayers and sufferings. In the end these are the works that will follow us into everlasting life (cf. Rev 14:13). We will realize in awe how the word of God, the Truth, makes us free (cf. Jn 8:32.36), regardless of external circumstances, of inner trials, and of the influence of the world around us, which attempts to diminish the fullness and beauty of God's kingdom within us.

Dialogue
With the
Eternal One

The Good Shepherd

"I am the good shepherd; I know my own
sheep and they know me" (Jn 10:14).

L ord,
in a mysterious way,
what you are saying to us
rings true with what we feel within.
We know when it is your voice we hear
and when it is not.

Thank you for having compared us to sheep
as they are so good and docile.
You are like a mother
who never fails to recognize
the innocent child in her son gone astray.
You give us courage,
because you believe in our goodness.
For this we thank you.

Our whole life is an adventure of love.
You believe in our love,
and we should and want to believe in yours.
You lead us, Jesus.
You guide those who already know and follow you
as well as those who don't yet, but one day will.

Jesus,
you are the world's only great leader.
No one deserves this title but you,
the good shepherd who lays down his life for his own.
But how conscious of this are we?
We can't fathom it completely.
Often our eyes are blinded,
we are concerned only with matters of this world,
and we forget to be thankful to you.

Jesus,
you are with us,
making us hear your voice.
Your voice awakens us:
We want to follow you.

You Call Us By Name

Jesus,
on Easter morning,
you appeared to Mary Magdalene.
You call her by name.
You have forgotten the life she left behind her:
her troubled past, her sins.
You call her.

Do you call each of us in the same way?
Once we have decided to love you,
do you forget our past too?
Do you call us too by name?

How can we continue to worry
about our failures
our past,
our sins?

Jesus,
are you not the same now,
as you were then?

Your Design of Love

L ord,
    what a desert surrounds us at times.
But we will get there; we're on the way.
We do not know how long our journey will be.
But we do not want to live
as if we will remain here forever.
Each day we travel a little further;
we rest and resume the journey the following day,
drawing ever closer to you,
though we know not our final hour.

Lord,
you promise all things
to those who ask with faith.
Grant that we may arrive only on the day
in which your plan for us is fulfilled.
Grant this to everyone we love,
and to all people,
so that soon we will all meet again,
united with you
and with your mother and ours
when the evening of this precious day,
life itself, has set.

Foretaste of Eternity

My God,
allow me the joy of knowing that
what we often aspire for in heaven
has already begun here below,
because living in the Church
is to live in eternity already,
even though in time.

Jesus,
help me to give you joy
by comprehending the greatness
of the gifts you have left us,
and by making these gifts known to many.
So that in the next life,
where sacraments and hierarchy will be no more,
we may not regret having understood too little
how heavenly were your favors
and divinely enlightened your teachers.

Jesus Wept . . .

Jesus was "troubled in spirit" and he "began to weep." The gospel says it (Jn 11:35.33).

Jesus!
Your weeping consoles us.
In your tears we find our own.
You are patient with us and with our tears,
because you have wept yourself.
Wherever you see tears, you recognize yourself.

And you,
so self-assured, eternal,
unchangeable and blessed,
experienced distress in your human soul.

Thank you, Jesus,
for your passion and for your death,
but also for those other episodes
that make you feel so close to us
in our every hesitation and confusion.
It is then that we think of you.
You recognize yourself in us and live in us.
And there you continue your passion
for the salvation of all people.

Sources

The selections of Chiara Lubich's writings in this book have been newly translated from the following publications (numbers refer to page numbers in this book, followed by the page number in the original):

Scritti Spirituali/1 (L'attrattiva del tempo moderno), Città Nuova, Rome, 1991:
18:276; 26-27:252; 37:238; 38:236,239; 39:236; 49:275,276; 50:277; 53:274; 54:274, 277; 55:275; 56:276; 57:276; 72:256; 73-74:251; 79:232; 80-81:232,233,234,235; 82:235; 89:263; 91:263; 92:254; 93:263; 94:264; 95:264; 116:252; 123-124:250; 144-145:246; 146:248; 172:246-247; 173:246

Scritti Spirituali/2 (L'essenziale di oggi), Città Nuova, Rome,1997:
19:14; 20-21:11; 22-23:134; 24:214; 25:49; 28:90; 29-30:127; 31:186; 32:77; 35-36:121; 40:95; 46:180; 47:34; 48:20; 58:36; 65-67:161; 68:171; 69:91; 71-72:72; 77:193; 78:167; 83:78; 84:39; 85:105; 86:67; 90:37; 96:62; 99-101:12; 101-103:164; 103:110; 104:89; 105:81; 106:65; 107:59; 108:39; 109-110:35; 113:48; 119:56; 120:83; 125-126:66; 127:80; 131:102; 132:17; 133:198; 134:103; 135:196; 136:209; 139:86; 140-141:57; 142:54; 143:43; 147:69; 148:53; 149:79; 157:84; 156:75; 157:28; 159:16; 160:32; 161:29; 162:40; 163:168; 164-165:18; 169-170:101; 171:197; 174:47

L'Unità e Gesù Abbandonato, Città Nuova, Rome, 1984, 61:24-25

M. Cerini, *Dio Amore*, Città Nuova, Rome, 1991, 17:17-18

The following selections are taken from *Living City Magazine*:
43-45:May'99; 62-64:Feb.'97; 114-115:March'96; 117-118:Dec. '97

Other books by Chiara Lubich available from NCP

Christian Living Today
Meditations
ISBN 1-56548-094-5, 7th printing, paper, 168 pp.

Jesus: The Heart of His Message
Unity and Jesus Forsaken
ISBN 1-56548-090-2, 2d printing, paper, 112 pp.

May They All Be One
ISBN 0-911782-46-X, 7th printing, paper, 92 pp.

Here and Now
Meditations on Living in the Present
ISBN 1-56548-138-0, 2d printing, hardcover, 80 pp.

Christmas Joy
Spiritual Insights
ISBN 1-56548-120-8, 2d printing, hardcover, 64 pp.

A Call to Love
Spiritual Writings, Vol. 1
ISBN 1-56548-077-5, 2d printing, paper, 176 pp.

When Our Love is Charity
Spiritual Writings, Vol. 2
ISBN 0-911782-93-1, 2d printing, paper, 152 pp.